I BEAT PORN

HOW I WON THE BATTLE AGAINST PORN ADDICTION

ANGEL PEREZ

Copyright © 2015 by Angel Perez

I Beat Porn
How I Won The Battle Against Porn Addiction
by Angel Perez

Printed in the United States of America.

ISBN 9781498457682

All rights reserved solely by the author. The author guarantees all contents are original and do not infringe upon the legal rights of any other person or work. No part of this book may be reproduced in any form without the permission of the author. The views expressed in this book are not necessarily those of the publisher.

Scripture quotations taken from the New Century Version (NCV). Copyright © 2005 by Thomas Nelson, Inc. Used by permission. All rights reserved.

Scripture quotations taken from the New International Version (NIV). Copyright © 1973, 1978, 1984, 2011 by Biblica, Inc.™. Used by permission. All rights reserved.

Scripture quotations taken from the Easy to read version (ERV). Copyright © 2006 by World Bible Translation Center (Bible Gateway.com).

Scripture quotations taken from the English Standard Version (ESV). Copyright © 2001 by Crossway, a publishing ministry of Good News Publishers. Used by permission. All rights reserved.

www.xulonpress.com

Dedication

I want to dedicate this book to my Savior, my provider, my strength, and my eternal Father. He is always taking care of me and has always been by my side, even in my darkest moments. He rescued me and gave me a new life and a new purpose. He is and will always be more than enough for me. I thank Him for giving me the motivation and the inspiration to finish this project. I love you Jesus!

Acknowledgments

First, I would like to thank my lovely wife Glenda Flores and my son Sebastian for being so patient with me during the production of this book. I couldn't have done this without you! Thanks to my family for always being there for me and supporting all my projects. I would also like to thank the great family of Dunamis Ministries, Pastor Adria Acevedo, and the entire staff for their unconditional love and encouragement. Special thanks to go to Irelis Santiago for her hard work on the initial editing process. Lastly, I want to thank all who supported me financially and spiritually during this amazing journey. Without your help, none of this would have been possible. God Bless you all!

Preface

There are several topics that you would probably never hear a preacher discuss on a Sunday morning service or during a weeknight Bible study. One of those "taboo" topics is pornography. Yes, the idea of hearing the word "porn" from a church altar makes many Christians squirm. Even though many people do not talk about it in Christian circles, this is a transgenerational issue that is affecting the Body of Christ worldwide.

What I have seen in my years as a believer in Christ and during my involvement in ministry is that many people in the Church do not know how to deal with this issue. There are two ways in which many Christians deal with the issue of porn in the church: they either ignore it, or they condemn it without offering any hope of healing and restoration. There are thousands of people sitting on our church pews, high schools, Christians and non-Christians, that want a way out from their addiction to porn, but they do not know how. So, is this a hopeless cause? No! I Beat Porn tells the journey of a young man who had been struggling with this issue since his pre-teen years and how he faced his fears, fought his battles, and received his amazing deliverance. Even if you have never been exposed to porn, this book will provide you with tools to help you get on the pathway to freedom from any addictive behavior. It will also help you be better equipped and more compassionate when helping others in this situation. Only God's grace could turn someone like Angel from a "porno boy" to an amazing husband, father, counselor and youth minister! You can be free too.

Rafael A. Mangual, MD
Assistant Pastor, Dunamis Ministries, Laredo, TX

Contents

Introduction xiii
The Subtlety of Porn 15
The Seduction 20
The Three Big Lies 24
The Aftermath 28
Double Life 32
The Danger of Idolatry 37
The Climax 41
Poisonous Relationships 46
Busted 54
Facing Embarrassment 59
The Church 66
Breaking Free 70
Created to Be Free 73
New Beginnings 81
You Can Do This 84
Final Advices 92
About the Author 99
Further Readings and Additional Resources 101

Introduction

In my years working as a youth minister, I have counseled hundreds of teenagers, young adults, and parents regarding the issue of pornography. It is not uncommon for me to have at least one or two cases of pornography addiction on a weekly basis. One day, while at a counseling session, I realized that the single question people always raise is, "How do I get out?" Most times, when people come to my office looking for help, they already know that they are wrong. They already know that pornography is pervasive and invasive. They do not need someone to tell them that they are sinning, but rather they need someone to tell them that there is *hope* and that there is a way out. This is exactly the purpose of this book.

I Beat Porn is a hope-based book that intends to provide biblical and spiritual tools for people to be delivered from their sexual addictions. This book recounts my testimony as a porn addict and how God, in his great mercy, rescued me. I will not only tell my story, but I will also unveil practical steps that helped me overcome pornography and its schemes. I want you to understand that you are not alone in your struggle. As you read these lines, there are thousands of people who are in the same boat as you are.

The focus of this book is to give you hope. God is more than enough for you, and he really cares about your situation. God sent his only Son Jesus to die for your sins. He was shamed on the cross so you could live a shameless life. He took your addiction upon him, and by his wounds you can now be healed and delivered (Isaiah 53:5). Your condition does not condition His love for you. His love will always be stronger than porn.

How to Use This Book

I will recommend that you use a Bible along with this book. As part of your recovery process, it is important that you put God's word in first place. The word of God was key in my deliverance. This is because the Bible contains the truth about God and His creation—us. Only through a thorough understanding of the truth of God will you be able to counteract the power of darkness. Always remember what 2 Timothy 3:16 declares, "All Scripture is God breathed and is useful for teaching, rebuking, correcting, and training in righteousness" (NIV). May the Lord bless you as you start reading this book.

Chapter 1

The Subtlety of Pornography

The Beginning

Addiction to pornography is not one of those things that comes into your life through the front door. It does not come in an obvious way, it does not happen overnight, but it comes very subtly. For starters, let me just tell you that it does not begin as an addiction, but rather as a curiosity or as an innocent game. I did not start watching porn one day all of a sudden. It was more like a progressive process. Before it became an addiction, it was just a compulsive behavior, and before it was a compulsive behavior, it was just a habit, and before it was a habit, it was just a sporadic thing.

I was born in a loving Christian home with high moral standards. I was surrounded with ministry because my grandparents were serving as Bible teachers in our church. At the age of twelve, I decided to become a Christian and serve God with all my heart and with my entire mind. Everything seemed to be perfect until one day the unexpected happened. One of my classmates from school showed me a pornographic video at recess time. They thought the video was funny, and they took it as a joke. It was the most horrific and disgusting thing I had ever seen. I remember telling myself with anger and revulsion "This is just wrong!" Little did I know that those images would eventually stir evil feelings inside of me. It was something that would change the course of my life forever.

The Mind

After watching that despicable video I went home, and for some reason I could not stop thinking about it. I asked myself, "If this is so wrong, why am I thinking about watching it again?" An inner struggle between good and evil started that very day. Those images were stuck in my head like a nail hammered into a wall. The most dangerous thing about pornography is that it damages your brain and everything that it comprises. Of course, I am not necessarily speaking from a physiological perspective, but what I mean is that it corrupts your thoughts and consequently your actions. Our minds are like fresh cement. Everything that you place on it will dry and will be attached to it. That short video was now subtly contaminating my thoughts and my godly desires little by little. At that point, two thoughts were dominating my mind; the first one was "This is wrong," and the second was, "This is completely normal."

In the name of "being normal," pornography starts playing its tricks on the mind. I started to fall into the idea that it was normal. I figured, "Well, my friends are doing it. They are normal people. They are cool. They would never hurt me on purpose, so what seems to be the problem then?" The next thing I knew I was heading towards my computer with the idea of watching the video one more time because I was just "curious." "It's just one more time and that's it," I said to myself.

Recognizing the Strategy

The enemy's strategy is always subtleness. He likes to sneak up through the back door so you wont know he's there. It is not always easy to recognize the enemy's plan, but you need to strive to unveil his malicious plans. One of the ways he operates is by making you think that pornography is completely normal. It is no surprise that this is the most common perception in society nowadays. Society wants us to believe that porn is as normal as sex education. Some even stress that it is a contemporary form of art, and some even argue for its efficacy as a sexual therapy for married couples. However, we need to understand that this is not just society's perception of porn but also a subtle strategy from the devil to deceive believers. We must never fall into the idea that porn is normal. This is exactly what happened to me. Slowly but surely the enemy managed to trick me. I was now unconsciously defending porn as something completely natural.

The Bible

What does the word of God have to say about this matter? In Genesis chapter 3 we see how the enemy has been deceiving men with his subtle tactics from the very beginning. "Now the snake was the most clever of all the wild animals the Lord God had made. One day the snake said to the woman, 'Did God really say that you must not eat fruit from any tree in the garden?'" (Gen 3:1 NCV). In other words, the enemy was saying, "Did he really tell you this is wrong? I mean . . . it's just a fruit. It wont hurt you . . . Right?" Notice that he did not say, "Eat it! Because this is my way of depriving you from what God has prepared for you! Eat it and you will surely die!" Instead he just tried to make God look like an insensitive and selfish brat by saying, "He knows that if you take that fruit you will become just like him, knowing good and evil" (v5).

Do not let the enemy deceive you! His only desire is to distort the words of God and your godly principles. His only goal is to make sin the new "normal" in you.

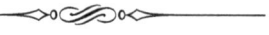

When we apply this word to our days with the issue of porn, it's the same thing. God tells you, "Hey this is wrong, and you know it," while the enemy whispers, "Hey! God just doesn't want you to experience this because he doesn't want you to have fun and enjoy life; God just doesn't get it. You have needs and you need to satisfy them. Go ahead!" Nevertheless, when we recognize the enemy's strategy, we become able to thwart his plans. Do not let the enemy deceive you! His only desire is to distort the words of God and your godly principles. His only goal is to make sin the new "normal" in you.

Chapter 2

The Seduction

The Talking Computer

After hours struggling with thoughts about whether or not I should go to the computer and find the video, I finally decided to go into my room and turn on the computer. I still remember that nervous anticipation—my heart was pounding and accelerating by the second. I felt a mix of feelings. I knew in my heart that I was about to take a huge risk, but at the same time I was filled with an inexplicable excitement. It was as if the computer could talk, "You're about to be amazed, man! This will blow your mind away." I went to the search engine and typed "porn" and then clicked "search," and that's when my entire life started to go downhill. As you may already imagine, the options were endless; of course this cannot surprise us since porn is one of the fastest growing industries online. I started viewing pictures, videos, and even movies. The more I watched, the more hooked I became. I even remember having images in my head of girls asking me to go to my computer as if it was some sort of blind date.

False Illusions

Porn gives false illusions and false pleasures. I literally felt as if the girls in the videos were real acquaintances. I used to picture them as friends and lovers at the same time. The reality is that it was all a *lie*. There was nothing real about those images—just fake love, fake affection, and fake sexual relations. Porn is just a distortion of the nature of sex, interpersonal relationships, and love. Porn dehumanizes and corrupts. Like I stated in the first chapter, the enemy likes to distort God's truth. In the same way, porn strives to distort God's truth about sex and love. I was now seduced by porn and its false pleasures. I was completely hooked.

Porn Is after You

Dr. Jose Colon, a dear friend of mine and a professional counselor who specializes in pornography addiction, states, "The problem is not that people are after porn, but that porn is after people." With all the advancements in technology, especially with smartphones, pornography is now more accessible than ever. People no longer have to access porn from a desktop computer or go to the store to buy a magazine. Pornography is now available at the palm of people's hands.

Social media, television, advertising, and YouTube are all filled with adult content material, making it harder for people who are dealing with this issue to be free from it. Likewise, I wasn't looking for porn, but somehow porn found me.

It is important to understand how serious this problem called pornography is. We must not be ignorant of the terrible predicament our generation faces. You, who are probably trying to break free from this trash, need to understand this as well, so you can be constantly aware and come up with a strategy to counter its attacks. Why? Because the truth of the matter is that we are living in a hypersexual culture, or what I like to call a sexually oriented culture, that unfortunately has disassociated sex from God.

I was so obsessed with porn that it was the only thing I could think of. Everything around me would bring forth an image or a video in my head. Even though I tried several times to quit watching it, the seduction was too strong. I was constantly struggling with sick and perverted thoughts that to some extent I could not control. My computer was now a hub of videos and pictures that would seduce me to the point that I became their slave. The power of seduction was so strong that, even though I knew I was heading to a living hell, I was willing to pay the price just to experience the temporary arousal and excitement of porn.

The Bible

What does the Bible have to say about this? Although porn can be very seductive and relentless when it comes to calling your attention, you must never forget that the power of God's love is always stronger. The love of the Father is the power that holds the world. The powers of darkness are no match to the mighty God we serve. Paul put it this way, "But God shows his great love for us in this way: Christ died for us while we were still sinners" (Romans 8:5 NCV). Simply put, God loves you right now just as you are! Think about it. It's not that we had to go through a rigorous religious rite so that God could love us, but even in our deathful state, God decided that we were worth saving. God is telling you right now, "You are worth saving because you are my son." God loves you, and therefore he wants to set you free. Let the love of the Father take over your life in this very moment. Let him love you; accept the gifts of salvation and grace today. Nothing can be powerful enough to separate you from his love (Romans 8:39).

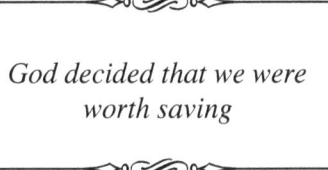

God decided that we were worth saving

Chapter 3

The Three Big Lies

No Escape

Like I stated earlier, the problem with pornography is that it messes up your brain, meaning that it distorts your thoughts and even your emotions. Since pornography is made up of lies, it is no surprise that its ultimate goal is to fill your mind with false ideas about God, yourself, and the people around you. The first big lie that the enemy tried to make me believe was that I had no escape and no hope. I remember listening to a voice deep within me that would say, "This is a dead-end road; there is no escape." When you actually recognize that you have a problem with pornography, that's when the enemy tries his best to bring a sense of hopelessness into your life. Of course, this cannot be further from the truth. The truth is that there is hope and there is a way out. Since I have always known the Word of God, I knew deep in my heart that I had good chances of breaking free from my slavery. It was that same hope that would hold me up in times of hardship and hopelessness. Thus, please do not believe the enemy and the thoughts he puts in your head. Remember, they do not call him the father of lies for nothing!

This Is Who You Really Are

The second big lie is, "This is who you really are," meaning that your addiction to porn has now become your identity. I really thought of myself as a sick, twisted pervert whose life was defined by the images I had seen. I remember classmates bullying one of my best friends (who also happened to be a porn addict). They called him "porno boy." Although this might sound funny for some, the truth of the matter is that this is very dangerous and of course depriving for one's emotional and spiritual stability. The enemy literally wants to label you as an addict. But you must remember that you are more than your addiction. The addiction might be part of your life for now, but it does not comprise your whole life. You have an identity. You have been created in the image and likeness of God. God holds your present and your future (Jeremiah 29:11).

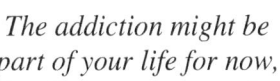

The addiction might be part of your life for now, but it does not comprise your whole life.

You Are too Dirty

The third lie is, "You are too dirty, therefore God does not want you." This is one of the most dangerous lies. The enemy wants you to believe that you are not worthy of God's grace, that you are not worthy of his forgiveness or His presence. This was the lie that affected me the most. I remember not wanting to go to church because I was too impure. Whenever I would go to church, I feared that God would strike me with a thunderbolt or something because my mentality concerning God radically changed. Now, instead of seeing God as loving, merciful, and compassionate, I saw him as an angry, hateful, and insensitive God who did not want anything to do with me because of my predicament.

The Bible

What does the Bible have to say about this? The Bible states, "No temptation has overtaken you except what is common to mankind. And God is faithful; he will not let you be tempted beyond what you can bear. But when you are tempted he will also provide a way out so that you can endure it" (1 Corinthians 10:13 NIV). God does not provide temptation, but he does provide the way out. God understands what you're going through.

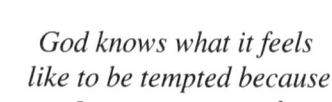

God knows what it feels like to be tempted because Jesus was tempted

God knows what it feels like to be tempted because Jesus was tempted. Our high priest, Jesus, cannot act with indifference before our struggles because he knows temptation, and he knows pain better than we do (Isaiah 53:3). Don't ever think that you are alone in your predicament. God does not care about porn, but he cares about you. He does not love porn, but he loves you, and he will do whatever it takes to get you out of your hardship.

You see, porn brings a lot of lies into your life, and only the truth shall set you free. What is the truth then? The truth is that you are not alone, that God loves you, and that you can be made free from porn. The enemy will always call you by your sin, but God will always call you by your name.

The enemy will always call you by your sin, but God will always call you by your name.

Chapter 4

The Aftermath

Frustration

Some of you may already know that after watching porn, your brain explodes with a plethora of chemicals that arouse your body. Consequently, you need to masturbate or act out what you saw in order to release and ease all that excitement. The problem is not only watching porn and masturbating, but the aftermath. Most people I have counseled admit their worst moment during the process of watching porn is the aftermath. Although orgasm brings a sense of relaxation and calmness, the truth is that, in the spiritual sense, this is not the case. Most people feel frustrated, sad, and even depressed. This was my situation. Yes, I was hooked up, but I would always feel guilty every time I had a setback. Even though my level of addiction was high, I still felt conviction in my heart that what I was doing was wrong and I was headed towards destruction.

Depression

I was like a walking zombie. I was very depressed, and at some point I really didn't want to live. I would only live to satisfy my sexual desires and my addiction. I would spend hours in front of my computer and hours lying in bed. Although I pretended to be active in church and at school, I was rotting away inside. My room was my prison, and my computer was my handcuff.

Temporary Commitment

Whenever I would watch porn and satisfy my sexual appetites, I would feel extremely guilty, to the point that I would erase all the pictures and videos from my computer shortly after experiencing an orgasm. I would cry out to God to set me free and deliver me from my torment, and then I would promise myself that I would never watch porn again. However, this was what I now call a *temporary commitment*. I would be clean just for a day, at most, and then relapse again. You need to be aware of this because a lot of people become very frustrated when they realize that they weren't able to keep their promise to themselves and God. In later chapters I will discuss how you can commit yourself to God and to yourself in order to be truly free and delivered.

The Bible

You need to understand that you are not alone in your struggle. As a matter of fact, you cannot escape from porn by your own strength. If you attempt to do this, you will be relapsing constantly. Instead, in moments of sorrow and distress, you need to hold on to God's grace. Look at what Paul said to the church of Corinth, "Three times I pleaded with the Lord to take it away from me. But he said to me, 'My grace is sufficient for you, for my power is made perfect in weakness'" (2 Corinthians 12:8–9). Do you know what this means? This means two things. First, it means that the undeserved favor of God is what you really need so you can be complete. Second, it means that this grace is unlimited and everlasting. God is telling you, "Rely on me; trust me; I can handle it; let me take care of you; you only need me."

Please pray this prayer and make it yours:

Lord, I acknowledge you as my Lord and savior. I know I have sinned, and I surrender my pride and recognize that it is only you whom I need. You are more than enough. Your grace is more than enough. Your power is stronger than my weakness. I repent from my sins, and I ask you to wash me clean. Please take control of my mind and my emotions. I know that I am weak but strong in your power. Holy Spirit, help me to rely on the power of God; activate the life of Jesus in me. Holy Spirit, guide and watch my steps. I need you, and I love you.

In Jesus' mighty name

Amen

Chapter 5

Double Life

The Sick Guy

My depression got so bad that I started to experience symptoms I had never felt before. I was so perverted and so depressed that I started vomiting, having headaches, sharp pains inside my head, and even high fevers. I was so confused and tormented that I started to believe that I was physically ill. By that time I was in tenth grade. I started to tell my friends and my teachers that I had a terminal disease and that my chances of living where low.

Of course, because I was well known at my school, everybody was very concerned about my situation. I even had friends visiting me at my house, but, it got worse. I convinced the entire school that I had leukemia. Yeah, you read that right—leukemia. I felt a lot of symptoms in my body, but everything was psychosomatic. Simply put, everything was a byproduct of the condition of my mind and heart. However, this is not the worst part. Although at school I was fighting against leukemia, at my house and my church I was just a healthy worship minister and a God-fearing youth leader. I was living a double life. At school I wanted to receive the support of my friends and the help of my teachers, while at the same time I wanted to keep my "godly" status and my "testimony" at church. I was trying to satisfy two needs at the same time. The truth was that I felt so dirty that I was just trying to compensate for my low self esteem by getting people to show me how much they loved me.

Church

Those were the worst times in church for me. I was playing in the worship band and also working as a youth leader. I was very engaged in activities and services in the church. People would love and support me and say great things about my family. Every time I would hear someone praising me, I would just feel disgust for myself, but I could not confess what I was going through by any means. I thought it was too risky to just confess the whole charade.

Whenever I tried to give someone a hint about my problem, my head would start thinking about all the possible consequences that would dramatically change my life. Therefore I just opted to continue living the lie in church, hoping that one day everything would just disappear. Simply put, my life inside the church was a lie. I was able to fool an entire congregation.

I was able to fool myself. But one thing was for sure; I wasn't able to fool God. He, better than anyone, knew my real condition. He knew what I was doing, but I was too stupid to realize that.

> *I was able to fool an entire congregation. I was able to fool myself. But one thing was for sure; I wasn't able to fool God.*

The Difficulties of a Double Life

Living a double life, while exciting to some extent, is definitely not an easy task. Maintaining two different identities seems to be impossible for some people. But the truth is that when you are so deep in sin, you become spiritually numb, and therefore you don't think about the consequences; deceiving people becomes your addiction as well. To live a double life means that you have to renounce to your real identity. I had to renounce what God said I was and what he wanted me to do on this earth. I had to adopt the enemy's plan for my life in order to satisfy my selfish desires. However, living a double life is difficult and tiring. I remember that I made up so many lies that I could not keep up with them. As you may already know, one lie creates another lie.

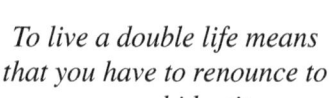

> *To live a double life means that you have to renounce to your real identity.*

I was creating my own trap and setting myself up to failure, but I was nonetheless committed to this lifestyle.

What about You?

Maybe you are experiencing a similar scenario. Maybe your story is a little less complicated than mine, or perhaps it's not. What is your reality right now? What is it that is holding you back from being honest with God, with yourself, and with the people around you? Are you living a double life? Are you striving every day to convince the world that you don't have a problem even though you know better? Here is the thing; sooner or later everything will come to light. One day you will get tired, and you will not have enough strength to continue manipulating your life every hour.

If there is one thing I have learned from my past experience, it's that being honest is the best thing you can do in times of distress. If you really want to be free, you need to be honest about yourself. Remember that we were created with only one body, one image, one personality, and one brain. We serve only one God who gave us one life, one purpose, and one destiny. Living a double life is a terrible mistake. Dare to live the way God wants you to live.

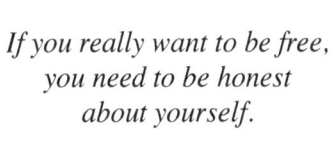

If you really want to be free, you need to be honest about yourself.

The Bible

James 1:8 says, "A double minded man is unstable in all his ways." In other words, you cannot expect to live an emotionally and spiritually stable life if you are living a double life. What does it means to be double minded? To be double minded means that you have no assurance of your identity. You do not know who you are, where you come from, or where are you going. You just live in the "here and now" without grounding your life on the truth of God. Being double minded also means that you want to live two different lives and satisfy two different needs. But you need to understand that God wants you to live the life he intended for you to live—a life filled with joy, love, peace, and self-control, and the power of his Holy Spirit.

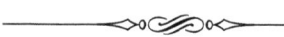

To be double minded means that you have no assurance of your identity. You do not know who you are, where you come from, or where are you going.

Porn only brings misery and heartaches. Its intention is to destroy that which is the most sacred, your relationship with God. Dare to be one minded. Dare to fix your eyes onto the one who wants to give you a brand new life. Fix your eyes towards Jesus. Dare to confess your double life, start destroying everything that is fake in your life, and turn to the God of truth. It will not be easy to start all over again, but the more time you wait, the more you will hurt other people and yourself.

Chapter 6

The Danger of Idolatry

"God Loves Me"

Why is it that every time you confront people with their sin, their first response is something like, "Don't judge me! God is a loving God, and he understands my weakness." Well, that was exactly my response whenever I heard a preaching or something that would address my pornography issue. I was so devastated inside that somehow I needed to ease my pain by making myself believe that God was ok with my condition. Let me just mention some of the arguments that I would make to myself:

1. "Every man has watched porn at some point in his life."
2. "I am just attracted to women, there is nothing wrong with that."
3. "Its better this way. I am not hurting anyone."

4. "God loves me no matter what."
5. "This is normal."
6. "God understands my weakness; his power is made perfect amidst of it."
7. "God will not send me to hell just because I get aroused with a woman. It's just part of the human biological makeup."
8. "There are people worse than me."
9. "If this is wrong, why does God allow it?"
10. "God's love outweighs my sin."

And the list goes on . . .

To be an idolater is not just to worship an image or a statue, but it is also to create your own image of God inside your head. People who do not want to face the reality of their condition will always find excuses to justify their behaviors.

People who do not want to face the reality of their condition will always find excuses to justify their behaviors.

In my case, I created a God who did not care about my condition. I created a God who would ignore the fact that I was an addict and considered me as "righteous." There is nothing more dangerous than accrediting false attributes to a holy and perfect God. Not only was I living a double life, but I was also being a total idolater. I was worshiping a figment of my imagination. Whenever I prayed, I prayed to my God and not to the God of scriptures. Whenever I talked to people about God, I was just talking about my God and not the God of scriptures.

The Truth

Pornography wants to distort the truth of God, the truth about yourself, and the people around you. Therefore, I think it is necessary that you see God not through the eyes of your predicament but through the eyes of the Spirit. The truth about God concerning your porn issue is as follows:
1. He loves you.
2. Since He loves you, he wants to set you free.
3. He does not love porn.
4. He is not ok with you watching porn.
5. He will never accept sin.
6. He wants to restore you.
7. He wants you to repent.
8. Porn represents slavery and not the abundant life of Christ.

As you can see, some of these statements are hard to swallow, even more so if you are actually struggling with porn. But it is only the truth that will set you free (John 8:32). To come up with your own ideas about God will only make things worse. Remember this, only a perverted mind can create a perverted God. The attributes of God are not from this world. He is holy, righteous, and eternal. None of these attributes is part of the nature of the human condition.

The Bible

There is only one true God. God is loving, merciful, eternal, and graceful, but the one thing that people often overlook is that he is righteous. You can never separate his love from his righteousness. Because he is righteous, he loves, and because he loves, he is righteous. Let me give you a simple example. God loves purity. He loves those who seek purity and rewards them. However, he cannot reward those who deliberately seek impurity through earthly pleasures and debauchery because that would be unfair for those who willingly seek righteousness.

Because he is righteous, he loves, and because he loves, he is righteous.

God is loving and righteous, but this does not end here. There is a way we can receive the justice of God. That way is through Jesus. It is only through Jesus that we can be justified before God. Whenever we decide to repent and look up to the author of our faith, Jesus, God the Father places his crown of righteousness over our heads. That is why Psalm 103:10–12 states the following, "We sinned against him, but he didn't give us the punishment we deserve. His love for his followers is as high above us as heaven is above the earth. And he has taken our sins as far away from us as the east is from the west" (ERV).

Chapter 7

The Climax

A Vicious Cycle

Addiction to pornography is a vicious cycle, and obviously my whole life revolved around it: Pornography-> Self Gratification-> Shame-> Guilt. As you can see, pornography is the beginning of this cycle. Pornography became my refuge and the only thing that would make me feel better. It was the only thing that would ease my pain and my anxiety. Somehow, pornography became my happy place.

The Conformity Stage

I was at the verge of insanity. My torment was getting stronger every day. I did not know what to do anymore. It was like swimming against the current. At some point I just got tired of swimming and let myself be taken away by the current. I got accustomed to being a slave. I adjusted my life to accommodate my addiction and I settled. This is what I called the *conformity stage*. It is when you no longer want to fight against pornography, and you just conform to the idea of being enslaved by it your entire life. Actually, it is when the idea of being a porn addict does not bother you anymore; it seems very normal. You understand that this will always be a part of you. This stage is a very dangerous one. The more you conform to your addiction, the more power it will have over you.

The Porn Lifestyle

Addiction to porn, like any other drug addiction, alters the individual's lifestyle. An addict cannot have a normal life even if he tries to. I realized that I was an addict because I simply couldn't live without consuming or even thinking about porn. My life was not normal at all. Everything I saw would trigger an erotic thought, even the most insignificant thing. Being without porn or something arousing felt like an unbearable torture. This is what I call the *porn lifestyle*.

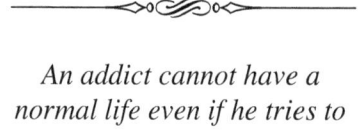

An addict cannot have a normal life even if he tries to

What do I mean by that? The first characteristic of the porn lifestyle is *secrecy*. Everything you do in order to get porn is secret. You even develop a malicious instinct to get what you want, when you want it, and where you want it.

You begin to think with cleverness and audacity about how to somehow disguise yourself as a normal person without blowing your cover. Nothing can stop you from getting what you want. The urgency to watch porn is so intense that you disregard any potential risks; you just can't think right.

The second characteristic of the porn lifestyle is *spiritual numbness*. At this point, your relationship with God has been completely broken. You do not pray anymore, you do not read your Bible, you do not worship, and you do not think about God at all. You don't even feel the need to repent anymore. In simple words, you turn your back on God. This is the most dangerous characteristic of the porn lifestyle because this means that now porn is your god, and everything in your life will revolve around it.

This takes us to the third characteristic; the porn lifestyle is *deceitful*. Basically what this means is that your life is based on pure lies. You have lied so much that you actually believe your own lies. It's somewhat like a neurotic person. You invent fantasies and then become infatuated with those fantasies to the point that you believe them to be part of your reality when they really aren't.

Deep down I knew I was wrong, but porn already had me trapped in its claws. It was crushing my soul, my mind, and my body, day by day without any compassion. I had no other choice than to bow down to it. Pornography became my everything, my god, and my world. Nonetheless, at this point I remember hopelessly crying myself to sleep every night. I was tired and in deep anguish. Only a miracle could save me from my living hell.

The Bible

Perhaps you are in deep trouble right now. Maybe you are at the climax of porn addiction, or far from it. Whatever the case may be, there is salvation and there is hope. It does not matter where you decide to direct your life, God will be always waiting for you with open arms. The Psalmist stated the following, "I could say, 'The darkness will hide me. Let the light around me turn into night.' But even the darkness is not dark to you. The night is as light as the day" (Psalm 103:11–12). You see, God is a God of light. In fact, He is the light (John 8:12). For God, there is no darkness. It does not matter how dark your life is right now, the Light of the world can light it up. He sheds light on your unresolved issues; he sheds light on your mind, your soul, and your heart.

It does not matter where you decide to direct your life, God will be always waiting for you with open arms.

The light of God can expose every dark area of your life. Imagine you are in a pitch-dark room all alone, scared, and without any visibility. Imagine there is no one there to hear your cry. You are desperately calling for help. You want to get out of the room, but you can't see the way out, and every attempt to escape is futile. You are just stumbling with everything in your way. All of a sudden, this guy comes into the room with a huge flashlight, pointing the light straight to your face and leaving you almost blind. Then he starts to light your way until you are able to see the exit. That is exactly what God wants to do with you.

However, I need to warn you about something. Light sometimes can hurt and be a little uncomfortable. Have you ever been in a dark room when, all of a sudden, someone turns on the light? What happens? You feel a quick but sharp pain in your eyes. This happens because the eye muscles contract so less light can enter into the eyes. This sensation is so bothersome and unpleasant that you feel annoyed and even angry with the person who turned on the lights. Likewise, when God exposes us through his light, we might feel pain, embarrassment, and disgust because light exposes our secrets. However, you need to understand that God wants to expose your reality, not to mock you or to make you feel ashamed, but to restore you. It is not until we are exposed to that light that we are able to deal with our issues. I dare you to step out of darkness and let God expose you to His light. I guarantee that you will never walk in darkness again.

Chapter 8

Poisonous Relationships

The Distortion of Relationships

As I have stated before, porn distorts the truth of God. The pornographic industry is in the business of profaning everything that is supposed to be sacred, like sex, family, love, and church. In short, porn distorts relationships. What kind of relationships am I talking about? It destroys all of them—your relationships with your family, with your spouse, with God, with friends, classmates, and even with your coworkers. All of your interpersonal relationships can be distorted because of pornography.

For instance, I could not see a girl without lusting after her. I could not see a couple holding hands in a park without recreating an erotic scene in my mind. I couldn't even have a descent conversation with a woman without undressing her with my eyes. It was a chaotic and miserable situation. Even more disgusting was the fact that I could not concentrate in church because all I could think of was sex. When you reach a certain level of porn addiction, the way you look at the world changes entirely.

In my particular case, people were not human beings, but they were sex machines. This is because one of the main problems with porn is that it dehumanizes people. Porn portrays people as sexual objects, and it does not take into consideration their dignity. So, it is very common for people who are addicted to pornography to lose sensitivity towards other people's needs. It is common for them to reject people and healthy relationships.

The Loner

Since porn dehumanizes and distorts relationships, it is no surprise that most people who struggle with porn are often very lonely people. I like to call them "loners." I became a loner. I would isolate myself from my family, from my church, and from my friends. Why did I do this? First, I did not want for people to confront me or judge me. Second, I did not want to get busted. Third, I lost interest in relationships. I simply did not want to be with anybody. My only companions were my computer, my cell phone, and my collection of porn.

Another thing that happened to me during my loner stage was that I started to criticize people for no reason. People just started to bother me. I would find the most insignificant shortcoming and then mercilessly attack the person just because they pissed me off. I started asking myself, "Why does this person annoy me so much? I just can't stand him!" I was so angry with myself that the only natural response for me was to get angry with other people too. I was mad at life. I was bitter, so I started to hate people and to mock them.

I even started making fun of people from church and ridiculing the pastors and their sermons. I was driven by hate. Therefore, not only I was isolating myself from people, but I was also keeping them away from me by hating and belittling them. In reality, I was trying to compensate for my lack of self-esteem. I was trying to play the "everything is ok with me" game with everyone., but I was just fooling myself. Unfortunately, I was alone, not by choice, but because of porn. Porn isolated me from the world. Porn wanted full custody of my heart, soul, and mind. Porn just wanted me and no one else. I was engaged with porn. Once you are caught by porn, she will try to do whatever it takes to keep you under her dominion.

From Watching to Acting

Watching porn was not amusing for me anymore. There was no hype, no excitement, and no intensity whatsoever. It wasn't enough. I needed something more attractive, something that would give me the rush I felt in the beginning. The thing is that when you reach a certain level of porn addiction, you will want to put into practice everything that you see. Your addiction will go from fantasy to reality.

Your brain is tired of watching the same images. As a matter of fact, your brain has already stored up all those images. You do not need to watch a video in order to get aroused. You just need to log into your brain archives and there will be plenty of material to choose from. You will transition from being a watcher to being a performer. But, the real problem is this. How are you going to perform it? With whom are you going to perform? Of course, it is obvious to say that people that practice premarital sex with their partners will be more likely to try out some of the things they see. But, what about those who are not in a relationship? What would be the outcome for those who are addicted to porn, but have no one to act it out with?

The Desperate Stage

I know that judging by the header you are probably thinking of that guy in your youth group who is just desperate to find a girlfriend. You know what I'm talking about. That dude who is always eager to greet every single new girl that steps a foot into the church. I used to call those guys "vultures." Or who knows, maybe I am talking about you. Let's face it; at some point in our lives we have been desperate to find Mrs. or Mr. perfect. However, here, I am not talking about this kind of desperation. I am talking about a sexual desperation.

I was sexually desperate. I had such an intense desire to have sex with someone other than myself that I was willing to do whatever it took just have a sexual encounter with someone. Does this ring a bell to you? Have you ever wondered why most sexual predators, rapists, and even serial killers had been addicted to porn before perpetrating their crimes? (Ted Bundy's Interview with Dr. James Dobson 1989).

There were four things that I would fantasize about: 1) inflicting pain 2) having sex with a complete stranger 3) foot fetishes 4) orgies. My sexual urges were too strong for me to handle. I felt like a balloon ready to pop. I knew my situation was getting out of hand when I started to have thoughts about rape.

I even started to act like a stalker around girls. I was becoming a maniac. I just wanted someone to help me ease my desperation. I even remember being terrified by the idea that some day I would rape someone or that I would turn into a sexual predator. My situation was miserable. However, amidst my desperation, I would pray to God to deliver me from my predicament. I would cry out deep in my soul for mercy. I knew deep in my heart that only God could intervene in my life, but my heart and soul were too distant from him.

The Bible

The Bible provides us with a truth that can never be ignored. God created us in his image and likeness (Genesis 1:26). What does this mean? This means that just like God, we are emotional, rational, moral, and most importantly, relational beings. As human beings created in the image of God, we long for relationships. Even the most antisocial person in the world strives to be accepted and loved. We were wonderfully designed with a powerful microchip programmed to love, laugh, cherish, and find comfort in people. It is our nature to be relational because God's nature is relational. God is not an antisocial, selfish, and ignorant God who only cares about himself. On the contrary, the Bible teaches us that God so loved the world that he sent Jesus to die on a cross so everyone could obtain salvation through him (John 3:16). Therefore the basis for our relationships ought to be love. What kind of love? The kind of love that 1 Corinthians 13 presents:

> Love is patient, love is kind. It does not envy, it does not boast, it is not proud. It does not dishonor others, it is not self-seeking. It is not easily angered; it keeps no record of wrongs. Love does not delight in evil but rejoices with the truth. It always protects, always trusts,

always hopes, and always perseveres. (1 Corinthians 13:4–7 NIV).

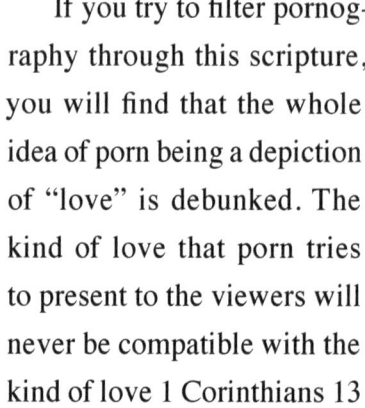

The kind of love that porn tries to present to the viewers will never be compatible with the kind of love 1 Corinthians 13 talks about because this scripture is a description of God's perfect love.

If you try to filter pornography through this scripture, you will find that the whole idea of porn being a depiction of "love" is debunked. The kind of love that porn tries to present to the viewers will never be compatible with the kind of love 1 Corinthians 13 talks about because this scripture is a description of God's perfect love.

The Greek word for this kind of love is *agape*. This word describes the perfect and infallible love of God for us. This love never fails. This love is pure. This love does not give up on us even in our darkest times. Only God can show this love.

It does not matter in what kind of situation you are in right now. It does not matter if you are addicted to sex or any kind of drug. It does not matter if you are a loner, or if you are sexually active with your partner, or if you feel that porn is all you think about. What matters is that you can understand that you were created in God's image. You have God's DNA. God longs for a relationship with you. You are his property. He is your creator and your designer. He wants to restore your relationships. He doesn't want you to feel alone, desperate, or confined to depression. He wants you to have an abundant life. He wants you to make new friends and enjoy life. But, remember that first you need to restore your relationship with him so he can restore your relationships with others.

Chapter 9

Busted

Toxic Routine

As I continued living my miserable life, my fears grew stronger and stronger. What was I afraid of? I was afraid of getting busted. I was afraid that one day somebody in my church would find out about my addiction. I was afraid that I would never be close to God again. I was afraid of turning into something that God never intended me to become. I was afraid of life. I was afraid of ending up alone in my misery. I was terrified of disappointing my family. But, I think that my biggest fear was disappointing God to the point that he would never love me again.

I continued to pretend everything was fine, and I tried my best to keep my addiction a secret. You know, the thing about being a porn addict is that no one will ever find out about your condition unless you confess it. Since there is no physical evidence, you can pretty much get away with it. Addiction to porn hurts the soul of the individual, and only those with a spiritual awareness can detect when something is wrong.

So, remember the story about me being sick at school? The leukemia charade? Well, this kept on going for a while to the point that everybody was grieving because I had poor chances of living. Well, all this was just a terrible excuse for me to skip school and stay at home watching porn. Besides, I honestly enjoyed the attention. I would stay at home from the moment my grandparents left home, until six or so because that's when they arrived. I was so depressed that I didn't want to get out of bed. I was always tired and sore. I would be in bed for hours, grab something to eat, and then go to my computer and watch porn for at least four or five hours straight. It was the same toxic routine every single day.

An Awkward Moment

My mother was working in a beauty salon during this time. One day while she was working with a client, something prompted her to go to the house. She didn't know what was going on with me, but she was about to find out. I was in my room, but I did not lock the door. The next thing I knew, she had popped the door open, and there I was masturbating to a video. As you can imagine, she freaked out.

She started yelling at me hysterically, "What are you doing? What happened to you?" I started screaming and crying. My mom started insulting me, and I don't blame her for this.

I got down on my knees and started screaming, "Forgive me mom, I'm sorry!" I remember telling her, "I'm sick; I'm sick, mom!" It was the most embarrassing moment of my life. I could not believe what was happening. After years of living in secrecy, my own mother finally busted me. Can you think of anything more embarrassing than that?

My mom, crying at the top of her lungs yelled, "I will go to your school and find out what's going on." And that's when I lost it! She was about to blow up my entire scam. She went to school and talked to one of the teachers. She asked her about my progress in school. I will never forget what the teacher responded, "He's trying his best under the circumstances."

My mother skeptically asked back, "What circumstances?" At that moment I knew I was screwed.

The Turmoil

As you can imagine, my mother was devastated, I was embarrassed, my family was confused, and my classmates and teachers were not too happy with me. The entire school was outraged. The school board had an emergency meeting to discuss my future. The majority of the teachers and school personnel were arguing for my expulsion, and some were even thinking about pressing charges against me. While all of this was going on, I could only remember being in a state of shock. I was mentally and emotionally paralyzed.

For most of my life, I had been considered to be a role-model student by my teachers, my family, and my church; I was a student with academic excellence and outstanding conduct. Now, I was being judged and hated as a liar, a pervert, and scum.

At that time, I had 282 absences in my senior year. Needless to say, that's an automatic suspension. There was no way I could have graduated. First, I committed academic dishonesty. Second, I did not fulfill any requirements from any class. And third, I actually did not learn anything in the last two years of high school. So, the school's principal wanted me to retake eleventh and twelfth grade and to offer a public apology. Those were very hard times. Who would have thought that a few pornographic videos could cause such mayhem? Certainly, porn is capable of doing this and much more. Remember, porn's goal is to destroy you. It does not take into consideration your ethnicity, religious background, or social status. No one is exempt from its attacks. It will do whatever it takes to entice you and bring shame into your life.

The Bible

The word of God teaches us that everything that is kept in darkness will someday come to light (Luke 8:17). Pornography teaches you to live a life filled with secrets, lies, and fantasies, but the reality is that sooner or later you will be busted. Someday your charade will be discovered. In my case, I couldn't confess my problem, but God, as an act of mercy, used my mom to expose my sin. However, you do not have to go through the same situation. You do not need someone to come and violently force you to confess your sin. You do not need to go through the kind of embarrassment I went through. Today God is giving you an opportunity to open your eyes and confess. God already knows everything you are going through, but God has also given you something called free will. You have the power to decide whether you will live in darkness or you will live in the light.

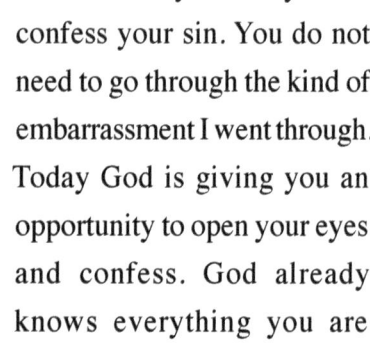

You do not need to go through the kind of embarrassment I went through. Today God is giving you an opportunity to open your eyes and confess.

Paul, in his letter to the Ephesians, tells us, "Live as children of light. For the fruit of the light consists in all goodness, righteousness, and truth. Find out what pleases the Lord" (Ephesians 5:8–10 NIV). Paul challenges us to live in the truth. The truth always brings blessings, but lies only bring condemnation, misery, and spiritual death (Romans 6:23). At times it seems easier to keep lying, but telling the truth, although difficult, will bring forth the restoration that you need. Only the truth shall set you free! (John 8:32)

Chapter 10

Facing Embarrassment

Troubled Times

After my mother discovered what was going on, things got pretty dicey. I did not know what was going to happen. I think everybody was astonished by the news. I just started to imagine the numerous consequences my actions could create. I thought, "Well, they will kick me out of school. I will never graduate from high school. I will never go to college. My family will despise me forever. My church will shun me, and God will forsake me for good. My life is simply over."

I could not think of a more horrifying time than that one. That day when I got home, I was trembling with fear because I did not know what to expect when my grandparents fond out about the news. My grandparents have always been people of great integrity. They are people who fear God and have always been involved in ministry. They are my role models in life. The idea that I could hurt them because of my dishonorable behavior terrified me. When my grandparents arrived at the house, I could not even look up to their faces. I was so ashamed that I just wanted to disappear from the face of the earth. My heart was pounding heavily. I was hyperventilating, and my hands were sweaty. It was as if I was next in line to be executed.

Balm of Peace

To my surprise, when I spoke to my grandparents, they were very understandable. Of course they were sad and shocked, but they did not beat me up like I thought they would. Instead, my grandfather said this: "Nothing will ever change; we love you." After many trials and hardships, these words were like a balm of peace covering my head. That moment gave me a chance to take a deep breath and do anything except to cry and sob.

School Dilemma

After much debate between the school council and my mother, they finally came to an agreement. The school counselor advocated for me entering a rehabilitation program from the city's mental health hospital. She said that I was suffering from a major depressive disorder and that the school didn't have the right to expel me because of my condition. She definitely saved my butt!

According to the agreement, I had to be under psychiatric treatment, finish all my late assignments, and take special tests in order for me to graduate. Some of my teachers didn't want to see me anymore. The truth of matter is that some of them really hated me. I really do not blame them at all, especially an English teacher that one day I fooled by making her believe that I had a stroke. I remember entering into the classroom and faking a twisted lip as if I had a facial paralysis. I was limping and everything. When she found out about the whole scam she got pretty upset. She was the one who wanted to press criminal charges and everything. Thank God, I had two teachers who really helped me in my predicament. They were very compassionate and willing to go the extra mile for my success. It was very embarrassing.

Still, the embarrassment never faded away. I spent almost a month struggling to see people to their face. I would literally walk looking down the entire time. This was just the beginning of a long restoration journey.

Crazy Doc

I was admitted into a mental health hospital in my hometown. I was scared to death! I kept telling myself, "Maybe I am crazy after all." It was a harsh season indeed. However, my mother took me by the hand during the entire process. She was very supportive and caring.

I remember waiting to be assessed by a psychiatrist. While we were waiting, I saw many weird things happen. I was face to face with people who had real issues. Some of the patients were in psychotic states. It was horrendous. I saw a teenage girl being treated for deep wounds in her arms after an anxiety attack. She turned out to be a cutter who had been suffering from major depressive disorder for years. Another guy who was seated right next to me had tried to kill himself and was hearing voices in his head. I just wanted to flee that place as soon as I could. It was a horror show.

After a few hours waiting for a doctor, they finally called us in. This doctor started to ask random questions. He then gave me a questionnaire to fill out. "Are you hearing voices? Have you ever attempted suicide?" You know, the usual stuff. But what happened next really marked me forever.

The psychiatrist asked me, "What seems to be the problem?"

I replied, "I am addicted to porn."

He said, "That's it? Many people watch porn. That's nothing to be worried about."

When he said that, I was outraged. It turned out that the doctor was the crazy guy! He told me that if I wanted to quit watching porn I should do it because of my religious beliefs, not because it will be harmful or out of the ordinary. He said that what can be harmful for me can be beneficial for others; simply put, it's normal. But since I was depressed, they prescribed me medications to balance out my brain chemistry. I tried to take them, but the side effects would leave me like a walking zombie. I just could not do it. I refused to take the medicine and to believe that I was depressed.

Needless to say, what the doctor said really shocked me. I wasn't expecting him to give me a magic pill that would solve my problem, but I at least wanted him to recognize that I was in serious trouble. He didn't think so, and this is exactly what's going on in our society. We have become so desensitized to porn that even some mental health professionals are completely indifferent about its dangerous, hazardous, and behavior modifying consequences.

Friends

Now it was time for me to face my friends. Honestly, I really didn't want to see them at all. Some of my friends from school knew me as a Christian. Others were active members of my Bible study club at school. They knew everything about me except my struggles as a porn addict. Imagine the kind of pressure I was about to experience. One day, four of my closest friends from school visited me at my house. When they saw me, their first response was to hug me and to weep with me. It was so comforting to know that regardless of my condition, they were willing to show unconditional love and respect to me. That day we laughed, and we had a great time together. I asked them to forgive me, and without hesitation, they did. My healing process was becoming a reality. Little by little, I was getting back on my feet again. That moment showed me just a glimpse of God's great love and mercy for me.

The Bible

The enemy will always try to mess up your dignity, but God will always turn your shame into joy. The Psalmist put it this way, "You changed my sorrow into dancing. You took away my clothes of sadness and clothed me in happiness" (Psalm 30:11 NCV). God is willing to change your shameful past into a glorious present. But, how can your shame be turned into joy? Only through Jesus. Jesus was ashamed, mocked, and ridiculed at the cross so you could now live with honor. Jesus changes your meaningless past into a meaningful present and future. Isn't that great? It does not matter what you have done, Jesus lifts you up to live an honorable and righteous life.

Would you declare this today?

You have changed my shame into honor. You have changed my meaningless past into a meaningful present and future. You were ridiculed so I could be praised. You were mocked so I could be respected.

You took my pain and my sufferings. Because of you, I am alive. Thank You Jesus for taking away my shame.

Chapter 11

The Church

Fear of Discrimination

You may be wondering: "What role did the church play in this situation?" The truth is that my church at that moment could not do anything for me because neither my family nor I said anything to the leadership. Why? Because I was too afraid of being discriminated against. The reason I am dedicating this chapter to the role of the church in my situation is because, just like me, I know there are a lot of people who are scared to confess their problems to their leaders; they fear prejudice or the possibility of being shunned by their congregation. Unfortunately, even leaders and pastors keep their mouths shut because they are afraid of loosing their jobs. At the time, I was a worship leader and a youth leader. I really didn't want to tell anyone, but at the same time, I knew I wasn't walking in integrity before God. Therefore, I decided to quit ministry. I knew that if I confessed everything to the pastorate, they would cut me off and put me in ministerial isolation. I figured that maybe it was better to quit on my own rather than to be thrown under the bus by the entire leadership.

Intimidation

Was my decision wise? Not at all. It was foolish and immature. I should have told them what was going on, but this is exactly how a lot of people think. Nevertheless, you need to remember that intimidation is the enemy's number one tactic when it comes to your deliverance. He will try to keep you away from having a healthy restoration process. Secrecy will always be a hindrance to your deliverance. It does not matter if you are a leader or if you are a parishioner, confession is always the best route to take. God will not leave you alone in the process. He will not put you through shame before men.

Time for a Break

Sometimes we need to recognize when it is time for a break in ministry. I resigned from all my duties at church and started attending as a regular member. It was my time to receive and not to give. It was my time to get back on my feet. Many people started asking me why I wasn't playing the guitar anymore, or why I wasn't leading the youth group. It was a constant bombardment of questions, and my answer was always the same: "I'm just taking a break. This is temporary." Of course that didn't stop nosy people from asking me the same questions every single week, but at least I would always give them an answer.

The Bible

The Bible says in 1 John 1:9 that "If we confess our sins, he is faithful and just and will forgive us our sins and purify us from all unrighteousness" (NIV). Note where it says *"he is faithful."* God is faithful, and he will always do what is right at the right time, at the right place, and with the right person. He cannot make a mistake. However, that does not necessarily mean that the church will always do what is right. That doesn't mean that pastors are perfect. It means that the only one who is capable of always doing the right thing is God. Therefore, you ought to trust him in the middle of your process. Put your trust in God, and you will never be disappointed. It is good to trust people in your church, but it is even better to trust the head of the church, Jesus. Do not fear the disapproval of

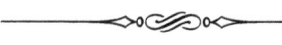

God is faithful, and he will always do what is right at the right time, at the right place, and with the right person

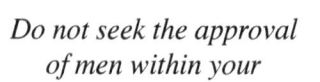

Do not seek the approval of men within your church, but rather seek the kingdom of God.

people. Do not seek the approval of men within your church, but rather seek the kingdom of God. Seek to be right with God and God will make sure to reward you in public (Matthew 6:4).

Chapter 12

Breaking Free

The Cravings

I would strive every day to be porn free. With the help of my family and my closest friends, I continued working on my deliverance process. One day at a time, I trusted God for freedom. But, just like in any other drug rehabilitation program, there were times when I had the *cravings*. The *craving stage* is where most people tend to relapse. It's when you feel an uncontrollable urge to watch porn or to have sex. Your mind blocks, your heart rate starts to rise, and you get anxious. You get desperate, and you might even feel short of breath. Literally, your body wants more porn. It's as if your brain is saying, "Hey dude! What happened with that thing you used to watch? I need it! You need it! We need it!" Yep, your brain has created what are called *neural pathways*. When you watch porn, your brain explodes with a plethora of chemicals known as neurotransmitters. These brain chemicals can alter your mood, your stress levels, and your arousal levels. Therefore, you are not only dealing with porn, but you are also dealing with your chemically dependent brain as well. In short, you are addicted to your own brain chemicals.

The Relapse

I had several relapses along the way. It is the most frustrating thing you can ever experience. Every time I relapsed, I would feel miserable and hopeless. I remember getting very angry. I would even hurt myself by hitting punches against the wall or hitting myself in the face. You might say, "Isn't that too extreme?" Yes. But when you are that frustrated, you just want to die. You don't really care about yourself anymore. I cried to God, "Please God, no more, no more!" It was heartbreaking because I knew I was disappointing God, my family, and myself.

The Easy Way

I did not know what to do anymore. I was desperate. One day, while watching porn, the enemy whispered to my ear, "There's an easy way to end your misery." The enemy started to put suicidal thoughts in my head. To be honest, it seemed like the best option at the moment. I was truly considering ending my life. I simply thought that was the only way I wasn't going to disappoint God or myself anymore. A sense of hopelessness came to my heart once again. I started to see my recovery from a distance. It was easier going back to porn than going back to my restoration process. Being porn free seemed like a fantasy rather than a reality. The enemy was playing his best cards on me.

The Bible

This is what the word of God has to say about this matter: "I tell you the truth, everyone who lives in sin is a slave to sin. A slave does not stay with a family forever, but a son belongs to the family forever. So if the Son makes you free, you will be truly free" (John 8:34–36 NCV). In this journey called restoration, you will have up and downs. Please, do not feel guilty or distressed because you had a setback. What you need to understand is that you are a son of God through Jesus Christ. Your life now belongs to him. You are part of his family forever, and nothing can or will ever separate you from His relentless love (Romans 8:39). He will not disown you just because you had a relapse. You are no longer a slave to sin. Jesus, the Son of God, has set you free. If you had a relapse, ask God to forgive you, accept his grace, stand up, and move on. This is no time to cry and feel self-pity. This is time for you to stand strong in God and put your trust in him. He already made a way for you to be truly free, through Jesus.

If you had a relapse, ask God to forgive you, accept his grace, stand up, and move on

Chapter 13

Created to Be Free

Enough is Enough

For four years, I had struggled with porn. I was fed up! I came to a point where I said, "Enough is enough! I have been praying to God to make me free. I confessed my wrongdoings. I had to face embarrassments and deal with depression. It is over. Until today I am a porn addict." It was somewhat like an epiphany. For the first time, I was angry with porn rather than with myself. I realized that being a porn addict was not what God intended me to become. After all, no one grows up saying, "I want to be porno boy some day." I felt a confidence and a power that I had never felt before. It was time for me to change.

It All Starts with a Decision

Great changes come through great decisions. Nothing will ever change in your life unless you start making important decisions. Life works based on decisions. If you want A's on all of your tests, you have to decide to study more. If you want money, you need to decide to get a job. If you want to have a family some day, you need to commit to a serious relationship.

Great changes come through great decisions

Likewise, if you want to see changes in your behavior, you need to decide to make changes in your habits. If you want to live the life God intended you to live, you will have to decide to get rid of porn as soon as possible. Nevertheless every decision needs commitment. If you really decide to be free, you need to commit your heart and soul to that decision; otherwise it will not produce any results. Decide to make a change today. Your deliverance is just a decision away.

Action Plan

Once you have decided to make a change, you need an action plan and a strategy for your restoration process. You may have the desire to change and may have already made a decision, but if you don't come up with an action plan, you will be constantly relapsing. What do I mean by a plan?

I've come up with a threefold action plan called *Restoration Action Plan (RAP)*. You can use this as a starting point and modify it according to your own particular needs. The RAP consists of three elements: *time management, relationships, and education.*

Time Management

Time is a precious gift given to humanity, but yet it is the most underestimated. How well you manage your time will determine the effectiveness of your plan. Perhaps you have heard the old adage "time is money." Well, we use money to make investments and produce an income. Similarly, you have to invest your time in a way that will produce positive outcomes.

What should you invest your time in? First, I recommend that you start investing your time in your community. Look for things to do in your local church, in your youth center, or simply by going for a stroll at the park, grabbing a trash bag, and picking up some garbage. Second, talk to your pastor and let him know that you want to work in ministry. It could be at the parking lot, welcome staff ministry, cleaning the restrooms, or any number of jobs in the church. Third, go out a little. Invite some friends to the movies. Have a get together at home with some burgers and hotdogs. Do things you have never done before or that you haven't done in a long time. Try new things! The important thing is that you start finding pleasure in things other than porn. There are a lot of ways you can enjoy life. Fourth, many people choose to take care of themselves through exercising. I remember I got a 3-month membership to a gym, although I only went 2 times. Nevertheless, working out is a great way to channel your energy and your stress. The whole point of time management is not only to keep yourself busy, but also to create new habits, discover new exciting and pleasurable things, and produce positive outcomes.

Relationships

The second element of RAP is relationships. This is often the hardest part to work with. This is where you have to make some important decisions. This is where you have to decide who will be part of your life and who will not. We all have people we care for in our lives, but they are not necessarily beneficial to our restoration process. I recommend that you take some time and think about your most influential relationships. It could be a friend, a boyfriend, a girlfriend, or even a relative. For this period of time you need to get rid of any person who isn't helping you to get delivered. For instance, if you have a friend who is always online being lazy, does not have a job, and likes to watch R-rated movies, that is not a person you should hang out with for long periods of time. Remember, there's nothing more important than your RAP.

Anything that represents a threat to your process should be taken out of the picture.

Also, you need to cultivate new relationships. Church is a great place to start doing this. Go to every fellowship event, every retreat, camps, or services. Church is a place where you can worship God while making valuable connections that will encourage you to grow spiritually and emotionally. This is a time where you can learn how to relate and communicate with people in a healthy way. Remember that for a long time porn had distorted your concept of healthy relationships. Therefore, it is important that you give yourself the opportunity to grow socially in a healthy environment.

Education

Education is the third element of this plan. What do I mean by education? Simply, it is a willingness to learn new things. For instance, when I decided to change my life, I started reading self-help books, devotionals, and Bible studies about purity. I also got interested in leadership books. I would talk to people who could contribute to my intellect and my spiritual life. I was committed to becoming someone great.

I wanted to know more about managing my life wisely and responsibly. Therefore, I looked for resources that could help accomplish that. Your rehabilitation process must be a time to learn. You have to learn new things about life, yourself, the world, and God. There are people who choose to learn a new language. There are others who choose to learn how to play a musical instrument. There are others who want to learn more about their condition. Sometimes people even enroll in college just to prove to themselves that they are capable of overcoming their fears and hindrances. Whatever may be the case, the important thing is that you are able to reinvent yourself through education. Education will always be present during this action plan. You need to learn how to manage your time while making valuable and meaningful relationships. Education never ends.

The Bible

"The Lord is the Spirit, and where the Spirit of the Lord is, there is freedom" (2 Corinthians 3:17 NCV). The Holy Spirit is the one who will give you the freedom you need. He wants to be your helper and your guide. The same Spirit that raised Christ from the dead is the same Spirit that wants to live in you. But how can you receive the Spirit inside of you? The day you acknowledge Christ as your Lord and Savior, that same day the Holy Spirit will come to dwell in your heart. The Holy Spirit wants to work in your character, emotions, and in your thoughts.

However, you need to understand that the Holy Spirit is a person, and like any other person, he desires relationships. He is not a blob of power hovering over the skies. He is a person. He wants to communicate with you. He wants to help you through this process. The Holy Spirit is the one who can empower you for success in life. He is the one who can lead you beyond your physical and mental borders. You don't have what it takes to stay strong and overcome porn. Your flesh is too weak, but the Spirit of the Lord will always be stronger than any addiction. This is why it is so important to establish a relationship with the Holy Spirit.

The Consequences of This Relationship

The greatest thing about this relationship is that it brings forth what the Bible calls fruits. A connection with the Holy Spirit produces love, joy, peace, patience, kindness, goodness, faithfulness, gentleness, and self-control (Galatians 5:22–23). These are the fruits of the Spirit. We are not capable of bearing these fruits unless we establish a strong connection with the Holy Spirit. What does it mean to have a relationship with the Holy Spirit? It means to:

1. Have total dependency on him.
2. Talk to him.
3. Listen to him.
4. Follow his orders.
5. Let him love you.
6. Let him heal you.
7. Walk with him and acknowledge him in all your ways.
8. Respect him.

Surrender your life to the Holy Spirit. Only in him, you will find true freedom and rest for your soul. Only through his divine intervention, you will find restoration. Remember, where the Spirit of the Lord is, there is freedom (2 Corinthians 3:17). Make sure he's in your heart today, and your heart will be truly delivered to better live the abundant life Christ wants you to live.

Would you pray this today?

Holy Spirit, I surrender my will, my thoughts, and my emotions to you. Help me overcome my fears and my weaknesses. Only through your divine intervention will I be healed. Only in you is there restoration. Put my life in order, and help me become more like Jesus. I know you live in me. I will give you the opportunity to do whatever you need to do in my life from this day forward.

In Jesus' name,
Amen

Chapter 14

New Beginnings

Celebrate Your Success

Rehabilitation takes time. It will have its ups and downs. Nevertheless, I want to advise you to celebrate your successes. Now that you are working on your habits through the RAP, I want you to celebrate every porn-free day. Sometimes we are too hard on ourselves during the process of recovery. We are too quick to condemn ourselves whenever we have a setback, but for some reason, we never tend to praise our own efforts when needed. Celebrating porn-free days will give you the motivation and the drive you need to continue with your rehab journey. This reward system will stimulate you to be more self-conscious about your thoughts, your habits, and your progress. How can you celebrate? The options are endless. Buy yourself a nice gift, cook yourself a nice meal, or go to a fine restaurant. Throw a random party with your friends, go to the movies, or go for a road trip; you name it! What matters is that you keep track of your progress by celebrating your success.

There is Always Hope

Where there is life, there is hope. I encourage you to hold on to that hope. Remember that life is a God-given gift, and you need to make the most out of it. Porn is just part of your past and nothing else. Now you need to keep moving forward. There's still a lot ahead of you. This is your time to enjoy life. This is your time to meet new friends, travel, study, work, fulfill your dreams, and grow as an individual. It is a time of new beginnings. Don't let anyone or anything ruin this new season for you. You have come a long way. You have conquered many obstacles. You have overcome your fears and your weaknesses. Today the sun shines brighter than yesterday. Hold on to that hope. Don't give up. Keep pressing on. Your victory is closer than you think.

Where there is life, there is hope.

The Bible

The book of Lamentations gives us a tremendous lesson about new beginnings:

"The steadfast love of the Lord never ceases; his mercies never come to an end. They are new every morning; great is your faithfulness" (Lamentations 3:22–23 ESV). Both his mercies and his love are endless. They will never run out on you. Isn't this great? God has decided to give you a fresh, new start every morning.

Today you might be suffering. Today you might be distressed. Today you might be in deep sorrow. But tomorrow, if you are able get out of your bed, it means that God is giving you a new opportunity to make things better. The mere fact that you are breathing and reading this book right now is proof of his great mercy and love.

Our God is the God of new beginnings! He will never give up on you. He will always be waiting for you with open arms to embrace you with his grace. Every day God gives you is a new chance for you to become the person he intended you to be. It's a new opportunity to see changes. It's an opportunity to see miracles happen. Life itself is a miracle. There are people all over the world who didn't wake up this morning. If you are still alive, thank God for his mercy and love. Thank him for the precious gift of life.

Chapter 15

You can do this

ACTS

Besides the action plan, RAP, I came up with the acronym *ACTS*. I'm sure it will help you get back on track whenever you have a relapse.

Admit it
Confess it
Tear down your giant
Seek help

Admit it

The letter A in our acronym stands for *Admit it*. Whenever you have a relapse you will try to make up excuses for it. You are so deeply frustrated that it feels like the best option for you is to ignore what happened. You will try to cover it up.

However, the best you can do is to admit that you had a set back. You have to admit you made a mistake and that you did something that led you to watching porn again. Acknowledge what you did so you can deal with it as soon as possible. However, let me warn you, admitting your mistake is not the same as getting on a *guilt trip,* rather it's about having *self-accountability.*

A *guilt trip* is when you can't stop condemning yourself for your actions. Getting on a guilt trip will only impair your ability to move on and continue with the rest of the steps in this acronym. You can't waste your time thinking about the things you could have done to avoid your relapse. What is done is done. You need to get over it and move on.

Self-Accountability is when you take responsibility for your actions. Instead of ignoring the fact that you made a mistake, you actually acknowledge that you had something to do with your relapse. However, self-accountability is not accompanied by guilt. Whereas guilt trip condemns you, self-accountability calls you to redeem yourself.

Confess it

The letter C stands for *Confess it.* Confession is simply the disclosure of information to an individual. You need to tell somebody about your problem. When you confess your problems, you are breaking the silence. I once heard a former porn addict who was a minister say, "Tell me how big your secret is, and I will tell you how strong your chains are." Confession is what eventually will lead you to your restoration.

Confession is a crucial step for your rehab process. It cannot be skipped. First, it takes the weight off your shoulders. Another person can be part of your struggle. You don't have to suffer alone. Secondly, another person can hold you accountable. It is important to always have someone to watch your back. Accountability always sets boundaries. You will think twice the next time you want to go back to porn. Thirdly, that person you are accountable to can give you a broader view of your problem and can give you more insights as to how to overcome your addiction.

Confession is a big step. I know is not as easy as it sounds. That is why it's important for you to choose the right person. Up next, I will give you some important qualities this person must possess in order to be considered a good confidant.

1. *Listener-* this person must be quick to listen and slow to speak. The whole idea is to have someone you can confess your problems to, not someone who will give you a three-hour lecture.
2. *Emotionally Stable-* by this I mean that you can't run to a person who deals with the same issues as you. Also, don't choose a person who is too dramatic or too sensitive to deal with bad news. Believe me, the last thing you need is someone busting in tears in front of you, making you feel guilty and miserable.

3. *Mature-* the person must have something wise and intelligent to say. A mature person will give you sound advice and practical tools to help you to succeed.
4. *Confidential-* you want to make sure the person you confess to is reliable and will not shame you by spreading your secrets to the entire neighborhood. One way I can distinguish if a person is a good confidant or not is if that person talks badly about people behind their backs with me. If someone spreads gossip about other people with you, most likely that person will talk smack about you as well.

Here is a list of possible people you can consider talking to:

- Pastor
- Youth leader
- Professional counselor
- Friend
- Anonymous support groups
- Teacher
- Family member
- Spouse
- Online support groups

Tear Down your Giant

Our next letter is T, and it stands for *Tear Down your Giant*. I remember that when I decided to get rid of porn, I had to make some radical decisions. I had to tear down everything that presented a possible threat to my restoration process. In my case, my giants were my computer, my cell phone, friends, and some habits. What does it mean to tear them down? For instance, I had to stop using the computer for a long period of time. That meant no more emails, no more chatting, no more live stream movies. In order for me to use the computer, I had to move it to a more visible area so my family could also see what I was watching. I also had to install accountability software to my cell phone and electronic devices. In addition, I had to terminate some relationships with friends who weren't the best influence at the time.

I recommend that you pluck out from the root anything that can hinder your growth and can become a stumbling block for your rehab. Do not bargain with your giants. You need to be radical. Your giants may come in many forms; you must recognize them and tear them down. Only you can do that.

Seek Help

The letter S stands for *Seek Help*. Most people fail this last step. Whether through embarrassment or ignorance, many tend to fall into the cracks and never receive the help and support they need to overcome porn. Seeking help is not a sign of weakness, but rather it is a sign that you have matured enough to recognize you have a problem. Those who are willing to seek help are more likely to be successful in overcoming their addictions. You can't get rid of porn by yourself.

There are now many resources at your disposal. Many decide to seek help at their local churches, local counseling center, psychologists, and other professional routes. Others may even get into a rigorous reading discipline plan or get an accountability partner to supervise their progress. Whatever kind of help you look for, do it quickly before your problems worsen.

I would like to make a disclaimer. The ACTS acronym worked for me as a restoration process many years ago. However, every case is unique and complex in its own particular context. The ACTS is not an exhaustive psychological therapy or anything of that sort. It is meant to be a practical, down-to-earth action plan that seeks to help you focus all your efforts into winning the battle against porn.

I strongly believe that any person who is struggling with any kind of addiction should always have an action plan to wage a counterattack against their addiction. Wanting to be free without an action plan is just a futile wish.

The Bible

The ACTS acronym, if looked through a biblical standpoint, would be like this:

Admit it
Confess it
Tear down your giant

Seek God

The S now stands for *Seek God*. This was really the game changer in my story. Without the grace and power of God, I would have never been able to overcome my addiction. The Bible states in Matthew 7:7, "Ask, and God will give to you. Search, and you will find. Knock, and the door will open for you." (NCV). In this passage, Jesus is giving us the key to unleashing the powers of heaven. He is revealing to us what we should do in order to receive answers from God.

ASK = Ask, Search, and Knock.

God is always willing to pour out his blessings upon us, but that does not mean that we need to stay stagnant and wait for it to happen out of the blue. You need to *ask* God for your deliverance, *search* his presence in intimacy through prayer and reading of His word, and *knock* on the doors of heaven through worship and praise so the character and attributes of God can be exalted in your life. Only then, will you see the hand of God operating in your life like never before.

"If God wants to bless me so much, why do I have to ask for it? Wouldn't it be cool if he just did it?" There is a reason

God wants us to ask him. As human beings, we tend to be very self-reliant and self-centered. We think we know everything there is to know about life and ourselves. We think we can be in control of everything, including our addictions. However, God wants you to depend on him rather than yourself.

Your character is flawed. You don't have what it takes to be free. You don't possess power. Your finite mind is always subject to your own evil desires. We are prone to live independently from God. God loves when we ask him, because it means we acknowledge that only he has what we so desperately need. The peace that you are longing for is only found in his saving grace. The joy that your heart needs is only found in his presence. The self-control that you are striving to acquire through your own strength is only found in his Holy Spirit. And the love that can make you whole again is only found in Jesus Christ, the Son of God. Do everything possible to stay out of porn. Find professional help, read books, and get an accountability partner, but what ultimately has the power to change your life is the divine intervention of God. Seek him first, and everything else will be added to you (Matthew 6:33). If you really want to be free, just ASK him.

> *God loves when we ask him, because it means we acknowledge that only he has what we so desperately need*

Chapter 16

Final Advices

Stay Free

Strive to be porn free, not for a week, not for a month, but permanently. It will take time. It might not happen over night, but the sooner you start working on your rehab process, the better. I would like to reinforce the main idea of this book: There is hope! Don't give up. You can beat porn. It is possible to live a porn-free life.

Spread the Word

There are millions of people around the world who struggle with porn. Many will not recognize that they have a problem, but many others will. If you happen to know people who are struggling with this illness, help them. Perhaps you can teach them some of the techniques and ideas you learned from this book. Spread the word of hope. Tell them they can beat porn too. Raise your voice against its schemes and lies. Inform your community about the dangers and consequences of watching porn. By helping others overcome porn, you will feel a sense of accomplishment that will give you the drive to keep pursuing a porn-free lifestyle.

Run away from Temptation

Being porn free does not mean you will be temptation free. As long as you live on this earth you will be bombarded with opportunities to go back to your old lifestyle once again. Run away from these opportunities. You, better than anyone, know what causes you to fall. You know your triggers. Avoid situations or circumstances that would trigger the need to seek porn again. Do not engage in erotic conversations and double meaning jokes. Be careful with the usage of Internet. Be aware of the amount of time you are spending in social networks and avoid spending too much time doing nothing. Remember that porn is always looking for the right opportunity to strike.

Never Flirt

Please, never flirt with porn or with any material with a high sexual content again. Many people relapse when they try to prove to themselves that they are "porn free." Don't try to be super man or super woman. If you feel that you are over porn, good for you! Stay free, and stay strong, but don't flirt with it. Don't just go and log into a porn site just to check if you really overcame it. Remember that if you expose yourself to porn again, you run the risk of having a huge relapse and going back to the same old lifestyle, putting at stake everything you have accomplished so far.

Don't Be Lazy

Laziness is the number-one porn trigger. When you have "nothing to do" and you just lay on the bed daydreaming and pondering about your existence, that's when temptation comes and where most people surrender to porn again. This is why it's so important to have a proactive lifestyle. Manage your time in such a way that you would never give porn enough time to mess with your head again. Keep yourself busy! There is a lot to do.

Stop Making Up Excuses

Excuses are lies that are used to justify a behavior or a decision. Lies only satisfy the liar. Stop making up excuses. Many people try to blame others for their addiction. Many blame their parents, their socioeconomic status, and even God.

The fact of the matter is that you are the only person responsible for your predicament. Circumstances might have influenced on your decisions and your welfare, but ultimately you are the one who opted for porn. Now it's your time to set things straight and get back on your feet. People who accept their responsibility can get out porn faster than people who waste time lying to themselves and the people around them.

The Bible

"We must not become tired of doing good. We will receive our harvest of eternal life at the right time if we do not give up." (Galatians 6:9 NCV). Perseverance is the key to success. God created us to be resilient. *Resiliency* is the ability to withstand turmoil without becoming dysfunctional. It is also the ability to resist hardships without breaking apart and falling into a depressive state.

Paul, in his letter to the Galatians, reminds us of the importance of persevering in the way of righteousness. He instructs us to press on and never get tired of doing what is right before God. Doing the right thing, although difficult, will always bring its rewards. All of the advice and principles throughout this book are not easy to live out. As a matter of fact, there were times when I would get really tired of trying to do right without seeing the results I expected. Nevertheless, I would

Doing the right thing, although difficult, will always bring its rewards.

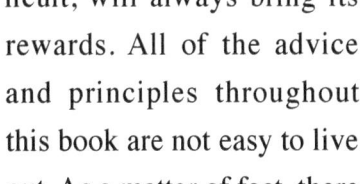

I would rather get tired trying to be free than get tired and still be enslaved.

rather get tired trying to be free than get tired and still be enslaved. I can assure you that if you persevere and do what is right, you will receive your reward.

Part of doing the right thing is to persevere in a relationship with God. Maintaining a strong relationship with your creator will not only satisfy your soul and give you a new purpose and a new way of seeing life, but it will also give you *eternal life*. This is the kind of reward we should all be seeking. This is the real reason we should never get tired of persevering along God's path. He promises eternal life to those who repent and put their faith and trust in Jesus. What you are experiencing in your life right now is temporary. Everything on this earth shall pass, but God and his Word will never pass (Matthew 24:35).

I encourage you to keep doing what is right. I challenge you to give your entire life to Jesus. He is the only one who can guarantee an eternity in heaven. He is the way, the truth, and the life (John 14:6). God wants you to be free from porn, but what he desires the most is your salvation, so you can live with him for all eternity. Our goal in life is to spend eternity with our master and hear him say, "You did well. You are a good and loyal servant. Because you were loyal with small things, I will let you care for much greater things. Come and share my joy with me" (Matthew 25:23 NCV).

Final Call

If you have doubts about whether or not you are saved. I want you to reflect on your life for a few minutes and pray this prayer:

God, I come before you in Jesus' name. I recognize I am a sinner. I recognize that I need a savior. Please forgive my sins and wash me clean. I acknowledge Jesus as my Lord and God. I acknowledge that he died on a cross for my sins and that he was resurrected on the third day. From this day forward, I commit my life to being your faithful servant. Thank you because I know I have been forgiven, and I am now your son/ daughter.

In Jesus' name,
Amen.

ABOUT THE AUTHOR

Angel Perez has been devoted to restoring, counseling, and disciplining young people for the past five years. He is the Youth Pastor at Dunamis Ministries in Laredo, Texas. He also serves as a Christian counselor for the adjacent community, where he specializes in porn addiction and substance abuse. From a very young age he proved to be talented at playing the guitar, which allowed him to tour around the world with prominent and very successful artists from both secular and Christian backgrounds. Currently, he's married to his wife Glenda, and together they have a baby boy named Sebastian. In his spare time, he's an active blogger and works as a musician, composer, and music producer. He holds degrees in music performance from the Puerto Rico Music Conservatory and in psychology and Christian counseling from the Liberty University in Lynchburg, Virginia.

Further Reading and Additional Resources

- xxxchurch.com
- Brooks, G. R. (1995). The centerfold syndrome: How men can overcome objectification and achieve intimacy with women. San Francisco, CA: Jossey-Bass Publishers.
- Harris, J. (2003). Not even a hint: guarding your heart against lust. Sisters, OR: Multnomah Publishers.
- Frederick, D. (2007). Conquering Pornography: Overcoming the Addiction. Enumclaw, WA: Pleasant Word.
- X3 Watch—Accountability software
- Neil T. Anderson (2000) *The Bondage Breaker*. Harvest Publisher. Eugene, Oregon.
- Stephen Arterburn and Fred Stoeker (2000) *Every Man's Battle: Winning the War on Sexual Temptation One Victory at a Time*. WaterBrook Press. Colorado Springs, Colorado.
- Lisa Eldred (2015).
- www.covenanteyes.com
- www.angelpitoperez.blogspot.com
- www.facebook.com/ibeatporn
- Colón, J. F. (2006). Auto-erotismo, un enfoque holístico para considerar en el proceso de consejería. Revista Paideia Puertorriqueña, http://paideia.uprrp.edu Universidad

de Puerto Rico, Recinto de Río Piedras Vol.1, Num.1
Año 2006

Carnes, P. J. (2001). Out of the shadows: Understanding sexual addiction (3rd ed.). Center City, MI: Hazelden